SMALLGROUP
ToolBox

DISCOVERING YOUR SPIRITUAL GIFTS

Ron Kallmier

CONTENTS

INTRODUCTION

Over the years the subject of spiritual gifts has stirred both interest and disagreement. During more recent decades there has been a wider acceptance across the Church of the ongoing importance of spiritual gifts, which are given by the Holy Spirit for the purpose of expanding the kingdom of God and building the maturity and wellbeing of members of the Church of Jesus Christ. Because you have chosen to use this book, clearly you have an interest in this important topic.

The world is going through a period of dramatic and unpredictable change. There is evidence of rapid expansion of the Christian Church in many areas of the world and worrying signs of its contraction in other areas, particularly the Western world. And this is just one feature of the global upheaval that is occurring during the first decades of the twenty-first century. In the developing world particularly, astonishing accounts of God at work through ordinary individuals are reported regularly. There is clear evidence that God is still pouring out His gifts on His people today. In fact, as we look carefully at the biblical texts we discover that each one of us has been given spiritual gifts which God wants us to use as He directs us.

Despite opposition, misunderstanding and human failure our God continues to release His Spirit powerfully into the lives of ordinary people all over the world to fulfil His purposes. Whether we live in the Western world or in another nation, it is important that we explore Scripture to understand the nature of our spiritual gifts. We need to be clear concerning the reason God, in His wisdom, planned long ago to entrust these special gifts to people like you and me.

This Bible study resource is based upon four key New Testament passages that provide insights into the apostle Paul's and the apostle Peter's teaching concerning spiritual gifts:

EPHESIANS 4:1–16
1 CORINTHIANS CHAPTERS 12–14
ROMANS 12:1–21
1 PETER 4:1–11

My prayer is that this resource will provide a helpful framework for your journey of discovery, both for you as an individual and for your group, as you consider questions such as: What are these spiritual gifts? What gifts do I have and how can I use them wisely?

There are three parts to this resource: First, there is an individual focus, guiding personal study and reflection. The second provides questions and suggestion for study of the Bible passages within a small group context. The final section offers some thought-provoking questions regarding the use of spiritual gifts in your Christian group, local church and in the wider community.

SUGGESTIONS FOR YOUR PERSONAL USE OF THIS BOOK

- There are many books on spiritual gifts available today that provide a more thorough (and more varied) look at this topic. This resource is designed to help individuals and small groups investigate what the Bible teaches on this topic and to consider how to exercise your spiritual gifts in ways that will bring honour to God, blessing to His people and benefit to those outside the church community.

- This booklet aims to give you greater confidence that God is interested in you, that He wants you to partner with Him in the work He is doing. It will be wise to set aside quality time for prayer and meditation on what comes to the surface as you read.

- If you are confused or unclear concerning your unique gift mix, it is often helpful to take some time with one or two close friends and discuss the matter with them. Of course, in small groups, this discussion can take place there.

- At the end of this booklet you will find an additional resource that was written by Selwyn Hughes on this topic (see the Appendix). Both individuals and groups may find that his insights stimulate helpful thought and discussion.

- In addition to the spaces provided in this study book, you may find it useful to have a small journal or notebook to record your discoveries or your thoughts or, perhaps, any questions you would like to raise in the group.

SUGGESTIONS FOR GROUPS WHO USE THIS BOOK

- If you plan to use the book in a small group, it is recommended that group members read all the relevant background notes, and spend some time in personal preparation. With our busy lives, this will be quite a challenge for many but the preparation will help to give maximum benefit to the group members.

- Spiritual gifts are not simply an interesting topic to be discussed; they are God's provision for His people. We should approach the topic humbly, and seek the wisdom and guidance of the Holy Spirit as we draw near to the outworking of God's mighty power.

Turn to page (37) for Notes For Group Leaders.

SETTING THE SCENE

WHAT ARE 'SPIRITUAL GIFTS'?

The words 'grace' and 'spiritual gifts' in the New Testament come from the same basic root word and that word means to rejoice or be glad.

In the passages of this study various terms are used to describe what we call 'spiritual gifts' in our English translations of the Bible. On occasions the word is simply 'spirituals', meaning spiritual matters. In Romans 12:6 and in 1 Peter we have the familiar word *charismata*. What we can be sure of is that these gifts are expressions of God's favour and empowerment, not just on those who carry them but on those we are called to serve with these gifts.

It may be a surprise for some to realise that spiritual gifts were not only given after the Day of Pentecost, when the Holy Spirit released His power on the band of believers. Earlier, the biblical accounts of the commissioning of a number of the prophets, such as Isaiah (Isa. 6:1–13); Jeremiah (Jer. 1:1–19); Amos (Amos 7:10–17) provide us with examples of God at work through the Holy Spirit in Old Testament times. We can then add the extraordinary spiritual endowment for the artisans involved in the building of the tabernacle (Exod. 31:1–11). Additionally, and interestingly, we have examples of people exercising a spiritual gift but only for a limited time, for example, Saul (1 Sam. 9–12). It appears that in Old Testament times spiritual gifts were given to a limited number of selected people.

The Day of Pentecost changed all that. Many Bible commentators identify the coming of the Holy Spirit in such a dramatic fashion (Acts 2) as the beginning of the fulfilment of the prophecy in Joel 2:28–32 where Joel prophesied that the Holy Spirit would be flooding the lives of all people, without regard to their status, gender or race.

'Then, after doing all those things,
I will pour out my Spirit upon all people.
Your sons and daughters will prophesy.
Your old men will dream dreams,
and your young men will see visions.
In those days I will pour out my Spirit
even on servants – men and women alike.
And I will cause wonders in the heavens and on the earth –

blood and fire and columns of smoke.
The sun will become dark,
and the moon will turn blood red
before that great and terrible day of the LORD arrives.
But everyone who calls on the name of the LORD
will be saved,
for some on Mount Zion in Jerusalem will escape,
just as the LORD has said.
These will be among the survivors
whom the LORD has called.'
New Living Translation

Peter (Acts 2) began with a defence of their behaviour and then broke out into a Holy Spirit inspired gift of preaching/evangelism. How powerful and effective this was!

JESUS AND SPIRITUAL GIFTS

A close examination of the Gospel accounts shows that Jesus operated in many of the spiritual gifts mentioned in the later writings of the Early Church. We can readily recognise gifts such as prophecy, insight (knowledge), healing, wisdom, teaching, pastoring and miracles, in the records of His life on earth. It is worth adding that we also see clear evidence of the fruit of the Holy Spirit (Gal. 5:22–23) in His life.

It was the power of God at work in Jesus that authenticated His teaching. His miracles pointed to God and went hand in hand with His inspired teaching.

If Jesus is the pioneer, the forerunner, of those who follow Him, we are called to imitate Him and, in some ways, exceed His actions (John 14:11–14), all to the glory of God. The gifts or endowments of the Holy Spirit become channels through which the presence and power of God can be felt and identified by believers and non-believers alike even in our times.

THE APOSTLE PAUL AND SPIRITUAL GIFTS

The apostle Paul did not set out to write a theology of spiritual gifts. Likewise, his aim was not to provide a 'how to' guide on spiritual gifts. In his letters to the Roman and the Corinthian Christians, and those believers in the church in Ephesus, he was addressing current issues of understanding and practice that were relevant specifically for believers in those important cities. The issues for Rome were different from those in Corinth and Ephesus, but each has provided us with very helpful insights into the apostle's understanding of the nature and functioning of spiritual gifts. When we study the various passages today, we do need to keep the culture and contexts of the original churches in mind as we study the text in his letters and as we apply what we find in our own situations today, so many centuries later. The same warning applies to our understanding the writing of Peter.

WHY SPIRITUAL GIFTS ARE IMPORTANT TODAY
Non-believers are blessed by spiritual gifts

In the Western world particularly, truth has become very fluid. This is especially true in the area of values. People do not have a problem if your 'truth' is different from their 'truth', but they may become defensive when you claim that yours is the only truth. For many, truth has become a point of view rather than anything solid or absolute. Beliefs concerning God and faith are treated exactly the same way. As a result, the best arguments in the world may leave our listeners stimulated but unconvinced and certainly uncommitted.

People of the twenty-first century are also very pragmatic. They want to know if something works and if it is good for them. As we have just noted, a strong argument may win a debate regarding faith or truth and yet leave the person unimpressed or even antagonistic. Yet if a sceptical person sees or hears evidence of God at work, this can be very attractive, opening the door of their lives for a more thoughtful consideration of the possible benefits of faith in God.

When Christians exercise their spiritual gift(s) for the benefit of others in the wider community under the guidance of the Holy Spirit, people are blessed and indifferent hearts can become warm.

Added to this desirable outcome, let's not forget that Jesus exercised gifts of healing and miracles to bless people who never responded to Him by becoming disciples, though of course we do not know what occurred later in their lives. There is a strong argument that Jesus blessed needy people simply because He expressed His Father's heart of compassion for needy people.

I have friends who regularly set up a booth in New Age festivals in capital cities in Australia. God works through them in healing, prophecy and words of insight. They have told of times when they have had queues outside their booth with people waiting to get in, some wanting explanations for their dreams, others wanting prayer for physical healing. For me, the most interesting comments are those of people who say that their booth has a different 'feel' from any of the others. The Christians at work there understand the culture, and give of their time, gifts and money freely, simply because God loves these people. A few come to faith but many are simply blessed with an intimate contact with the Holy Spirit of God at work through God's people. Who knows what will be the eventual outcome of the seed that is planted there? As in New Testament times, the *work* of God can open up the way for the *Word* of God.

Christians too are blessed by the appropriate exercise of spiritual gifts

In his first letter to the Corinthian church, the apostle Paul clarifies the purpose of spiritual gifts for the Church. They are 'for the common good' (1 Cor. 12:7). Evidently there were difficulties in the Corinthian church both in their understanding and use of spiritual gifts. These difficulties, whatever they were, did not lead Paul to tell the church to stop welcoming or exercising spiritual gifts when they met. To do so would have hindered the work of the Holy Spirit in some measure and the church would have been impoverished as a consequence.

There is no doubt over recent decades that spiritual gifts have been a blessing to many. Sadly, there are also examples of gifts being wrongly used or abused, but this should not cause us to 'write them off'. For my wife, Jeanette, and myself, spiritual gifts exercised by others have blessed us personally. At other times the spiritual gifts we have been given by God have provided us with opportunities to be channels of God's grace to others.

'NATURAL ABILITIES' OR SPIRITUAL GIFTS?

Many of us will have grown up in a family with other children, or perhaps we have children of our own. We understand that even with the same mother and father every child is unique. Individual uniqueness shows itself very early in life because this is part of God's plan and design. For a variety of reasons, some of us never uncover or appreciate all our unique qualities and potential. Yet God knows how He shaped us as His **works of art** (in the Greek, *poema* – see Eph. 2:10) and how He has prepared us for His unique purposes for each one of us. As we have already observed, this 'natural' potential can remain dormant, like a seed in the ground, but it springs to life when it comes in contact with the life-giving water of the Holy Spirit's presence and power. The gifts we are born with (which some may call 'natural gifts') become supernatural when they are energised by the Holy Spirit. Sadly, many people are unaware of their God-given potential, or simply write their gifts off as insignificant or unimportant. Life itself is a wonderful gift from God and every one of us has God-given potential that the Holy Spirit desires to release. I believe it was Abraham Lincoln who said something like, 'God must love ordinary people. He made so many of them'. You may like to consider Selwyn Hughes's thoughts on this topic. He wrote:

According to the Scriptures, before we were born, God's sovereignty was at work preparing us for our emergence into this world. The Psalmist said, 'You were there while I was being formed in utter seclusion! You saw me before I was born and scheduled each day of my life before I began to breathe. Every day was recorded in your Book' (Psalm 139:15–16, TLB). God shaped Jeremiah for his ministry saying to him, 'Before I formed you in the womb I knew you, and before you were born I set you apart' (Jeremiah 1:5). According to these and other scriptures (see Luke 1:16, Galatians 1:15) a Sovereign God is at work preparing us to contribute to His universe in certain well-defined ways. In each one of us God builds into our personalities at the moment of conception (so I believe) certain aptitudes and abilities which later, through growth and development, become observable. Once we become Christians, however, a spiritual transformation takes place in which the Holy Spirit regenerates our dead human spirits (see Ephesians 2:1) and brings us to new life and a new identity. Immediately we are converted at least one of our basic abilities (sometimes more than one) is harnessed by the Holy Spirit to become our specific contribution to the ministry of development in Christ's Body, the Church. There takes place within us, whether we feel it or not, an inner thrust, or if you like, a distinct motivation, which leads us towards a specific form of ministry in Christ's Body. This inner drive is what constitutes a basic gift. It is the heightening and intensification, or as some prefer to call it, the 'Christianising' of a natural ability in such a way that an individual finds himself or herself inwardly motivated to play a certain part in building up the Church.
A basic gift then is a spiritual urge or motivation, produced by the Holy Spirit, alighting and impinging on a natural ability so as to sanctify it,

and transfigure it so that it becomes the potential for a significant contribution in the ministry of the Church. It does not mean that every natural ability is taken up by God in this way but one, at least, most certainly is, enabling believers to play their part in the most wonderful ministry in the universe – maintaining the health and vitality of Christ's Church here on earth.

5 Insights to Discovering Your Place in the Body of Christ

(Farnham: CWR, 1982, 2001), pp.20–21.

SPIRITUAL GIFTS IN PERSPECTIVE

The nature and purpose of spiritual gifts can be summed up in this simple diagram:

God is the GIVER	We are His AGENTS	The receivers are BLESSED	God is GLORIFIED

Over recent decades many Christians have shown a renewed interest in spiritual gifts. On the whole, this is a very healthy attitude. However, if we view these gifts as something that builds our status and self-esteem we have missed the point badly. As the diagram above explains, we are God's agents; His fellow workers (1 Cor. 3:9).

Imagine a parcel courier boasting about the valuable parcel he was delivering to a wealthy individual. We would most likely say to him, 'What are you talking about? You are only a courier. You didn't buy this gift and it won't belong to you when you deliver it.'

A similar attitude to our Christian gifts can keep us humble and balanced in our understanding of this great treasure with which God has entrusted us. Whether natural abilities or unique miraculous spiritual gifts, they are a trust from God and we carry them for the benefit of others – for God's people and for other individuals to whom God chooses to send us.

How many spiritual gifts are there?

Over time Bible students have tallied up the spiritual gifts they can see mentioned in the New Testament and if you read the findings you will discover discrepancies in their totals. I believe a good argument can be made that there are many more spiritual gifts operating among Christians than are listed in the New Testament. Additionally, individual Christians have an even more numerous **mixture** of spiritual gifts, so agreement on the exact number of spiritual gifts is probably unlikely and unwise.

Christians may be inclined to identify certain gifts such as prophecy, healing and performing miracles, as the supernatural work of the Holy Spirit. Yet this view is a misunderstanding. It fails to recognise how much God rests on the less spectacular gifts also and, in so doing, can lead to a two-tier idea of spiritual gifts. Every individual has the innate potential to cooperate with God through His gracious gifts. When we fail to see God's hand in the ordinary as well as the extraordinary gifts we possess, we may feel so insignificant or unimportant that we sideline ourselves.

Whether our gifts are those that have been with us from conception or we have received them at a later stage of our Christian walk, God is the Giver of them all. His gifts are the way He has chosen to express Himself through us. These gifts equip us for *every* part of our daily lives. There is no sacred and secular life with God. All of life is the same to Him. We are reminded in Peter's second epistle that we have everything we need to achieve what God has in mind for us. How encouraging is that!

His divine power has given us everything we need for life and godliness through our knowledge of him who called us by his own glory and goodness.
2 Peter 1:3

IN SUMMARY

The number of spiritual gifts in which we operate is not what is important. What matters is that we acknowledge that God is the giver; that we are called and equipped with all we need to be His fellow workers; that those who benefit from these spiritual gifts are blessed; and that the glory goes to God and not us.

PRAYER OF PREPARATION

Thank You, Lord, that each one of us who follows You has been blessed with Your gifts that we can share generously with others. During our journey through the Scriptures and this book, give us further insights into our unique gifts and how You desire to pour out Your favour on others through us. Help us, like the young boy prophet Samuel, to always pray, 'Speak, for your servant is listening' (1 Sam. 3:10).

PART ONE

SPIRITUAL GIFTS
OF LEADERSHIP

FOCUS PASSAGE: EPHESIANS 4:1–16

PREVIEW

Over recent years there has been much spoken and written concerning the leadership gifts mentioned in Ephesians chapter 4. The apostle Paul recognised the essential function that leaders play in the life of the Church. There are three important consequences of effective spiritual leadership that Paul underlines in this chapter:

1. God's people are prepared for works of service
2. The Body of Christ (the local gathering of believers) is unified
   (that is: perfectly integrated, linked together, and completely equipped for God's purposes)
3. The followers of Jesus will grow in spiritual maturity through their knowledge of Jesus Christ

Plainly the function of the leadership gifts is to promote the health, spiritual growth, harmony and maturity of those the leaders serve. There is an ongoing tension here for those of us who have leadership roles in the Church. Gifted leaders attract people who want to identify with the leader's character or perhaps his/her vision or teaching. Some will seek to imitate their leaders, believing that they set a healthy example of how they should live. This is not wrong in itself but it can cause problems for both unwary leaders and their followers. Some common areas that Christian leaders need to guard against are:

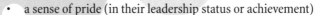

- a sense of pride (in their leadership status or achievement)
- a dictatorial attitude, as though leadership makes them somehow superior to those they lead

Jesus warned His disciples of these leadership traps on a number of occasions. Here are some examples you may like to investigate further:

MATTHEW 20:20–28; 23:1–12; MARK 8:31–39; LUKE 9:46–48; JOHN 13:1–17

Just as children need caring parents if they are to grow up healthy and balanced, so younger Christians need sensitive, effective leadership and pastoring if they are not to go astray in their Christian journey.

 ## PERSONAL EXPLORATION

1. Which Christian leaders (local, national, international, historical or biblical) have inspired you most by their giftedness, character and influence?

2. What qualities of these leaders have impressed you the most?

3. Do you consider that you fit one of the leadership descriptions in Ephesians 4:11–13? If so which one?

4. On what basis have you come to this point of view?

5. In what ways has this spiritual gift been confirmed in you by others?

STUDYING TOGETHER – EPHESIANS 4:7–16

1. There is a strong emphasis in the early verses of this chapter concerning the importance of strong, caring relationships and a bond of unity in the church family. How do leaders help make this happen?

2. From your understanding of the Scriptures, how would you describe the leadership gifts of apostle, evangelist, prophet, pastor (shepherd), and teacher?

3. What qualities should a spiritually gifted leader have, according to Ephesians chapter 4?

4. From your understanding of this passage, how can these very different types of leadership work in cooperation so that your church is growing, unified, mature and functioning effectively? Consider the different roles of each type of leader in your discussion.

APPLYING THE SCRIPTURES

1. With the pressures of modern life Christian leaders can become sidetracked into less important tasks. What do you believe are the essential tasks of spiritually gifted leaders today?

2. Based on the Ephesians 4 selection, what would be the evidence that spiritually gifted leaders are truly bringing a positive influence on individual Christians, small groups and your local church as a whole?

3. Which of the five leadership gifts are operating in your local church or Christian group? (Include outside leaders who have an ongoing influence on the church or Christian group.)

4. From your understanding of the selection in Ephesians 4, how can you discern between healthy and unhealthy Christian leadership styles?

PART TWO

SPIRITUAL GIFTS IN THE LIFE OF THE CHURCH

FOCUS PASSAGE:

I CORINTHIANS CHAPTERS 12–14

PREVIEW

Chapters 12 to 14 contain the most detailed discussion of spiritual gifts in the New Testament. Corinth was a Roman colony where many ex-legionary personnel were sent to provide a presence for the power of Rome in that area of the Greek peninsula. This was a multi-cultural context. It is probable that many of the new converts to Christianity struggled to disentangle themselves from their old cultural habits and lifestyle as they pursued a new life as followers of Jesus Christ. As a result of their situation, those of us who have lived since those times have been able to benefit from the apostle Paul's teaching on this significant topic of spiritual gifts.

It has not been helpful when chapter 13 has been separated by biblical teachers from chapters 12 and 14 as though they are unrelated. Spiritual gifts without the essential ingredient of *agape* love open us up to misunderstanding and even abuse of those wonderful endowments that God has given to each of us uniquely.

So essential is the connection between the exercise of spiritual gifts and love, that it is featured in each of the key readings in our study on spiritual gifts. Love directs our **heart** (compassion) and our **energy** towards the good of others, which is the heart of love as it is taught in the New Testament.

It is easy to become curious or impressed, or perhaps confused by the more spectacular or unusual spiritual gifts. Perhaps this was the difficulty that Paul was addressing in this letter to the church at Corinth. Spiritual gifts were being practised but not always in an appropriate fashion. Paul does not teach the church to stop using the gifts but, rather, he shows them how to release the gifts in the way that honours God – the better way.

Love is indeed the most excellent way (1 Cor. 12:31–13:1). It reflects God's heart to bless people simply because He loves them. Amazingly He has entrusted frail and failing people like you and me to be His agents in this task.

The source and purpose of spiritual gifts

> There are different kinds of spiritual gifts, but the same Spirit is the source of them all. There are different kinds of service, but we serve the same Lord. God works in different ways, but it is the same God who does the work in all of us.
>
> 1 Corinthians 12:4–6 (NLT)

The apostle Paul does not want us to forget that spiritual gifts come from God and are to be used under His direction. Paul stresses this thought by writing the same concept in the three slightly different ways. We know he was emphasising this point because he was using a literary style not unlike when we type something in bold or underline it today. By doing this he added *emphasis*, and the slight differences in each of the three parts also add some further *clarification*. We can be sure then that this is something not to be ignored – Paul considered it to be very important.

So why did he stress this point? The apostle Paul is making sure we do not overlook or minimise the fact that spiritual gifts are **all** to do with God. Yes, gifts will differ from person to person but each one of us is empowered by the Holy Spirit. Our gifts will be used for a whole variety of services, but it is Jesus Christ who directs how, when and where they are to be used. Each time we use our gifts under God's direction, God does far more than we could ever imagine.

Now to him who is able to do immeasurably more than all we ask or imagine, according to his power that is at work within us, to him be glory in the church and in Christ Jesus throughout all generations, for ever and ever! Amen.

Ephesians 3:20–21

Prophecy – more than about the future

Most human beings are curious concerning the future and so it is easy to focus on this aspect of prophecy. However, it is not the main focus of Paul's teaching, though he certainly endorsed its proper use. Paul's teaching in 1 Corinthians 12 addresses other important characteristics of prophecy – the speaking out of encouragement; the strengthening of faith; the building up (edification) and comfort of individual believers; the life of the church as a whole (1 Cor. 14:3). This function of prophecy comprises divinely inspired speech that lifts the human spirit and ignites the flame of hope. Positive, accurate prophecy is just as needed today as it was 2,000 years ago.

 PERSONAL EXPLORATION

1. Why not take the time to read the three chapters in one sitting or listen to a recorded version. Better still, read or listen to them twice – once in your preferred translation and then again in a modern paraphrase such as *The Message* or the *New Living Translation*. You may find it helpful to note down two or three things that have come to your attention as you have read or listened to these chapters. If you have a journal, you may prefer to write your thoughts there.

2. As we have noted previously, love is central to this whole section of 1 Corinthians. Take time to meditate on 1 Corinthians 13 and consider the reasons that motivated the apostle Paul to refer to the way of love as 'the most excellent way' (1 Cor. 12:31).

3. What discoveries or questions from these three chapters would you like to mention for discussion within your small group?

STUDYING TOGETHER –
1 CORINTHIANS CHAPTERS 12–14

1. 1 Corinthians 12:7–11: 'Usual' and 'unusual'
    In this passage the apostle discusses what we may describe as the more unusual gifts – prophecy, speaking in other languages (tongues), prophecy, miracles, healings and so on.

*   Why were these gifts so important for the Early Church?
*   How can they benefit local churches in the twenty-first century?

2. 1 Corinthians 12:27–30: Different people, different gifts
    These verses make it clear that spiritual gifts will vary amongst Christians. Each of us is unique.

*   Discuss the nature of various gifts mentioned. What part does each gift play in the growing work of Jesus Christ within the Church and in the wider world?
*   What may be the 'greater gifts' that the apostle mentions in verse 31?

3. 1 Corinthians chapter 14: Prophecy and 'tongues'

- Why does Paul value the gift of prophecy so highly? (vv.1–5)
- What do these five verses suggest is the main purpose of the gift of other languages ('tongues')?

APPLYING THE SCRIPTURES

1. Practically speaking, how can we encourage other Christians who believe they have no spiritual gifts?

2. 1 Corinthians 12:12–31: One body many parts
As we have noted, Paul chose the picture of the human body to describe how the Church is knit together. What do you believe was his main point in choosing this image? How can this picture of the Church as a healthy human body help you when you look at your own local church or group?

3. 1 Corinthians 12:25–26: Suffering and honouring
    Consider the significance of these two challenging verses for your
    group and your church. How would this look in real life in a local
    church? Do Christians in your group and local church sense this level
    of connection with one another?

4. What guidelines does your group suggest should be in place so that
    spiritual gifts operate helpfully and appropriately in your church?

PART THREE

MAINTAINING A HEALTHY ATTITUDE

FOCUS PASSAGE: ROMANS 12:1–21

PREVIEW
The flow from chapter 11:36 to Romans 12:1–8
The apostle Paul never misses an opportunity to remind us that God is at the centre of our lives; the centre of spiritual gifts. He takes up this theme again in an outburst of praise and worship before he introduces the familiar first verses of Romans 12.

> *For from him and through him and to him are all things. To him be the glory for ever! Amen.*
> Romans 11:36

It is because of who God is and what He is doing in our lives and in our world that we are called to lay all that we have and are before Him in willing surrender (Rom. 12:1–2). In this position of daily response to Him, His spiritual gifts will flow most freely and most purely in us and through us.

A balanced understanding of ourselves
With the Christians in Rome, Paul was engaged with a different culture and with different challenges to the Corinthian believers, and so his teaching focus is different from his instructions in 1 Corinthians 12–14.

Roman culture of the first century valued boasting. Now boasting did not mean the same as it does today. Perhaps it could be more like 'boosting' – raising the family's honour by one's actions and standing in the community. The effect was that people could easily get into a competitive attitude, seeking social standing and recognition rather than serving one another. Faced with this cultural pressure to put on a good show, Paul insists that believers should be realistic in their opinion of themselves (Rom. 12:3).

Paul encourages Christians to celebrate and accept their uniqueness and their different gifts and abilities. God has given each one different potential and different tasks, he reminds them. This is God's design. He values our uniqueness, so we should not be surprised when we are different from others. Diversity was always God's plan, and this includes spiritual gifts (Rom. 12:4–8).

Discerning your spiritual gifts and calling

Our gifts reflect God's calling on our lives. Remember that you are perfectly created and perfectly equipped for His perfect calling on your life.

Here are some clues that may help to identify your gifts and calling. The list below is intended only to give helpful pointers. The more of these points you can tick, the more confident you can be. Remember also that you will mature in the use of your gifts over time, and that God may call you at any time to use your gifts in new situations, so be prepared for this.

- Good fit (I find this easy and natural for me)
- I find doing this a joy not drudgery
- There is satisfaction and pleasure when I have used this gift, rather than relief that I got through it
- I have a passion for this ministry/task
- Doing this energises me rather than demotivates or drains me
- There are positive outcomes – I have success in using this gift
- Other mature Christians who know me well affirm that I have this gift
- I am aware of the presence and activity of the Holy Spirit, achieving far more than I could expect or do on my own

Reality check: In much of our daily life we have to do tasks that may not be in our comfort zone or preference. This can be true also in our specific Christian service. However, it is sad if we live our entire lives doing only those things that do not suit us, when we have genuine gifts and potential that are waiting to burst out and be expressed.

There can be a temptation to grasp the more visible and attention-gaining spiritual gifts even when they do not really suit us. Over the years many churches have suffered because individuals, including those in leadership positions, do not have the gifts for the task in which they are engaged. God calls us to use what He has given us. We are not accountable for what He hasn't given us.

Love must be sincere (Rom. 12:9–21)

One of a number of old folk traditions claims that dishonest sculptors in ancient Rome would fill any flaws in their statues with wax. Of course, a hot day could melt the wax and the deception would be clear for all to see. A genuine sculpture – one without defects – was a sculpture that was without (*sine*) wax (*cera*). This is sometimes claimed to be the basis of our word 'sincere'. Whether this is the true basis or not, sincerity does involve purity of motives, actions and words.

In these verses Paul unpacks what he means by sincere love towards God and others. Before we conclude that this is simply too high a standard we must remind ourselves that love like this requires the ongoing work of the Holy Spirit on our lives. He provides the motivation and the energy that makes this deepest form of love possible.

 PERSONAL EXPLORATION

1. Some Christians are unclear about their spiritual gifts. Others doubt that they have any spiritual gifts at all. Still others believe they have certain gifts when all the evidence suggests they do not. Here is a suggestion to clarify your own gifts:

2. Perhaps you have become aware yourself of one or more spiritual gifts that you use, or perhaps others have told you that you do operate in certain spiritual gifts. Write any of these spiritual gifts below.

3. Consider the possible evidence that was suggested previously under the heading, 'Discerning your spiritual gifts and calling'. Do your responses below back up your own thoughts or the encouragement of others?

	Not Me	Sometimes/Perhaps	Definitely Me
It is easy – natural for me			
Joy not drudgery			
Satisfaction, pleasure rather than relief when it is done			
I have a passion for the ministry/task involved			
It energises rather than demotivates or drains me			
Positive outcomes – I have some success in using my gift			
Other mature Christians who know me well confirm this gift			
Awareness of the presence and activity of the Holy Spirit, achieving far more than I could expect or do on my own			

4. If you are still unclear after considering this, please talk to someone you trust who has insight and integrity. You could also turn to the more detailed chart in the Appendix of this book.

5. Of course, it is important also to bring your uncertainty to the Lord in prayer for His wisdom.

STUDYING TOGETHER – ROMANS 12:1–21

1. How would you explain the nature of the various spiritual gifts that are referred to in these verses?

2. For what reasons are gifts such as service, encouragement, generosity and mercy included in the list of spiritual gifts? Do they appear to be too ordinary to be truly 'spiritual'?

3. From Paul's writing in this passage, how do faith and spiritual gifts operate together?

4. From your careful consideration of this passage, why do you believe that Paul's instructions to the church in Rome require supernatural empowerment and not simply greater human effort?

APPLYING THE SCRIPTURES

1. One feature of this selection is its focus on keeping our view of ourselves in balance. What practical steps can we take to do this if we are inclined to have an over-inflated view of ourselves?

2. What if we have the opposite problem and we feel inferior, inadequate or unimportant as a Christian?

3. Are there people in your group who operate in any of the spiritual gifts referred to in these verses? Take time to encourage and support one another. Why not spend time praying for one another for the more effective and courageous use of these spiritual gifts.

4. Which of Paul's instructions in this selection of verses would be the most challenging for members of this group?

PART FOUR

DON'T HOLD BACK

FOCUS PASSAGE: I PETER 4:1–11

PREVIEW

The apostle Peter wrote in very uncertain times for the Church. There was much persecution. Martyrdom was not uncommon. He wrote out of a sense of urgency. Time is short. It should not be wasted. The way he writes suggests that he believed that the end of the age was very close and so believers should not hold back in using the spiritual gifts that God had given them.

What he wants from his readers is a total commitment to the task at hand. He urges that his fellow believers should go all out in their service for God.

There are echoes of the parable of the talents (minas) recorded in Luke's Gospel (19:11–26). What our Lord gives us is not to be kept hidden but used for His benefit. Timothy also was urged by his mentor and spiritual father, Paul, to stir up the spiritual gifts that he had received after the laying on of hands and prayer (2 Tim. 1:7). Our spiritual gifts need to be stirred up. This is our task.

All of us have innate abilities which can be developed. The Holy Spirit may choose to anoint these in a powerful way when we follow Jesus Christ. Additionally God may add new spiritual gifts, and so increase or diversify our potential for service. Consider the apostle Paul as an example. He was undoubtedly a scholarly man and a gifted leader, and so Jesus Christ redirected his energies and used these abilities. But we discover he begins to move in miracles and healings and other apostolic anointing which only occurred *after* his conversion. He had a gift mix that God could use in a worldwide ministry, yet what really counted was that he was wholehearted in his commitment to Jesus. He too recognised that time was short for him and sought to make the most of every opportunity (Col. 4:2–6).

It is the same for us. We can be held back by insecurity, or busyness, or uncertainty, but often we have only one opportunity to touch another person with the blessing of God. So let's take note of the apostle's encouragement in this Colossians passage and take every God-given opportunity, whether it is to serve believers or non-believers. Let's not hold back, because by blessing others through our spiritual gifts we bring glory to God and bring people into His powerful and loving presence.

PERSONAL EXPLORATION

1. The apostle Peter began to unpack his potential in God only as he entered a deep friendship relationship with the Lord Jesus Christ. Is the flow of your life bringing you closer to God or do you sense you have drifted further away over recent months and years?

2. Take time to meditate on verses 7–11 thoughtfully and prayerfully. Note down any thoughts that stand out to you as you do this.

3. Of the qualities that Peter displays in these verses, which is the most appealing to you and which is the most challenging?

4. What have been the most challenging thoughts for you in these sessions?

_____

_____

_____

_____

STUDYING TOGETHER – I PETER 4:1–11

1. In verses 7–8, how do the qualities Peter mentions form a solid basis for using our spiritual gifts effectively?

_____

_____

_____

_____

_____

2. In practical terms, how can we faithfully administer God's grace in its various forms? (See verse 10.)

_____

_____

_____

_____

_____

3. Verse 11 – Followers of Jesus have to speak out for Him publically at times. This may be in a group of Christians; it may be speaking in a church service; or it may be simply one-to-one with a Christian friend or a non-believer. How can we speak as though it is God Himself speaking, without being arrogant or ignorant or misleading?

_____

_____

_____

_____

4. All of us have the privilege and responsibility of service at various times. When Jesus washed the disciples' feet He taught that this humble service was required of all His followers (John 13). What does humble service look like in a group of Christians together? Why is humble service so important when Christians meet together?

APPLYING THE SCRIPTURES

1. Verses 1–6 – Peter was aware that Christians who live righteously and who minister in the power of the Holy Spirit will stand out like lights in dark places. Spiritual gifts are one way that God can use to show that we are different from the world. Do any members of the group suffer because they live differently from those people with whom they associate during the week (family, work, school, neighbourhood, and so on)? If so, discuss how to handle this in a godly manner.

2. If the people to whom Peter wrote put verse 10 into practice in a very positive way, what evidence would you expect to see if you were an observer?

3. How can a constant reminder that your time is short (verse 7) motivate you so that you do not waste opportunities that God gives you? How can you balance this activity with a quiet confidence and rest in God (Psa. 46:10)?

4. What is the most significant challenge that you have learnt from the time you have spent studying spiritual gifts? Are any of the group members planning to make changes in their lives as a result of this series of studies?

NOTES FOR GROUP LEADERS

- It's up to you how you use this booklet – in any way that fits your own group best. While this booklet is designed to be covered in four small group sessions, feel free to take as many sessions as you believe are necessary to cover this important topic thoroughly.

- It is recommended that groups address **real questions** and **real issues** from within the group whenever this is appropriate. Sessions are not intended to be simply a theoretical discussion, but very practical. Please do not feel bound to follow the suggestions within this resource. Feel free to use what is appropriate for you and your group, to ignore the remainder, and to add your own ideas where these will benefit the group.

- In a healthy group environment individual uncertainties and concerns related to this topic should surface and this will stimulate frank and open exploration of the issues raised.

- Ideally group members should complete the series feeling clearer concerning their own gifts and be encouraged to use these gifts for the good of God's people and so bring glory to God Himself.

- By the way, we suggest you don't pressure anyone to be involved in the discussion if they appear unwilling. Make space for individuals to process their own thoughts and to consider what is being said by others.

APPENDIX: DISCOVERING YOUR BASIC GIFT by Selwyn Hughes

POINTS TO PONDER BEFORE ATTEMPTING TO DISCOVER YOUR BASIC GIFT

1. When you consider that Paul's listing of the seven basic gifts in Romans 12 follows on from his earnest appeal 'to offer your bodies as living sacrifices', it suggests that we ought to approach the whole subject in an attitude of prayerful expectancy.
   Dedication must precede revelation. Approach the matter after a period of quiet prayer and meditation, asking God to help you find and develop your unique ministry.

2. Remember that our natural talents and aptitudes are often the natural wrapping in which a spiritual gift may be deposited. God's gifts are often in line with a natural ability, and this is why our natural faculties often point the direction in which a spiritual gift may be used.

3. The absence of any particular gift does not excuse us from obedience to other scriptural commands. If a person does not feel he has a gift of 'giving', he is still expected to support the Lord's work financially. Similarly, if a Christian does not possess the gift of 'sympathy', he is still expected to show mercy and comfort those who are struggling (1 Thess. 5:14). This may raise the question: *'If we are all expected to do so much, where is the need for specific gifts?'* In some ways the Church is like a football field in which, although the players each have a separate function, all are expected to try and get a goal. Each one of us has a responsibility to work for Christ, but the major part of our work must be along the line of the spiritual gift (or gifts) which we have been given.

4. Confirmation that you have a certain basic gift will also come through the discernment of other believers. In fact, other Christians may see a gift in you long before you yourself are aware of it. It helps to prayerfully share with other Christians your conclusions before attempting to develop your gifts.

5. Just as deep settled peace pervades our beings when in the centre of God's will, so a feeling of great joy arises when exercising a basic gift. This inner joy is often a clue to the presence of a gift, and is often unconsciously communicated to those on the receiving end of your ministry.

6. Once you discover you have a basic gift, don't go around telling everyone, but adopt the attitude described by Paul in Philippians 2:3: 'Don't be selfish; don't live to make a good impression on others. Be humble, thinking of others as better than yourself. Don't just think about your own affairs, but be interested in others, too, and in what they are doing' (TLB). Watch for opportunities to minister your basic spiritual abilities and be quick to close in with what God is showing you.

INSTRUCTIONS

Use the thirty-five statements overleaf to help you discover your basic gift or gifts. Rate yourself with the following scale by writing the appropriate number in the corresponding number square (p.42). Ask yourself: 'Is this statement true in my spiritual life and experience?' Indicate your score in the appropriate number square on the chart over the page.

Greatly 3 Some 2 Little 1 Not at all 0

After you have completed the chart by rating yourself for each of the thirty-five statements, add the scores in each horizontal row. Record the number in the Total column. Your total score for each row indicates your level of interest in that particular gift. The highest scores may lead you to a clearer understanding of the basic spiritual gift or gifts which God has deposited in your life.

ALL GOD'S CHILDREN HAVE GIFTS

1. I enjoy presenting God's truth in an inspired and enthusiastic way.
2. I am always ready to overlook my own personal comfort in order that the needs of others may be met.
3. I find great delight in explaining the truth of a text within its context.
4. I am able to verbally encourage those who waver and are spiritually troubled.
5. I am able to manage my financial affairs efficiently so that I can give generously to the Lord's work.
6. I find it easy to delegate responsibility and organise others towards spiritual achievement.
7. I readily find myself sympathising with the misfortune of others.
8. I am conscious of a persuasiveness of speech when encouraging people to examine their spiritual motives.
9. I have the knack of making people feel at home.
10. I delight in digging out facts concerning the Bible so that I can pass them on to others.
11. I have a deep concern to encourage people towards spiritual growth and achievement.
12. I am cheerful about giving material assets so that the Lord's work can be furthered.
13. I am able to effectively supervise the activities of others.
14. I enjoy visiting those in hospital, or those confined to their homes due to illness or disability.
15. I am able to present the Word of God to a congregation of people with clarity and conviction.
16. I am happy when asked to assist others in the Lord's work.
17. I am concerned that truth should be presented in a clear fashion with proper attention to the meaning of words.
18. I am at my best when treating those who are spiritually wounded.
19. I have no problem in joyfully entrusting my assets to others for the work of the ministry.
20. I am able to plan the actions of others with ease and supply them with details which will enable them to work efficiently.
21. I have great concern for those involved in trouble.
22. I find myself preaching for a commitment whenever I present the truths of the Word of God.
23. I delight in providing a gracious haven for guests.

24. I am diligent in my study of the Bible and give careful attention to necessary research.
25. I am able to help those who need counselling over personal problems.
26. I am concerned over the question of financial assistance being available for all sections of the Church.
27. I am deeply sensitive to the needs of a smooth-running administration so that every phase of activity is carried out decently and in order.
28. I work happily with those who are ignored by the majority.
29. I find my preaching brings people to a definite point of decision.
30. I enjoy taking the load from key people so that they can put more effort in to their own particular task.
31. I am able to explain well how the Bible hangs together.
32. I am acutely aware of the things that hold people back in their spiritual development and long to help them overcome their problems.
33. I am careful with money and continually pray over its proper distribution in the work of the Lord.
34. I know where I am going and am able to take others with me.
35. I am able to relate to others emotionally and am quick to help when help is needed.

A CHART TO HELP YOU FIND AND DEVELOP YOUR UNIQUE MINISTRY

						Total	Gift
							(Please fill in after test is completed)
Row A	1	8	15	22	29		
Row B	2	9	16	23	30		
Row C	3	10	17	24	31		
Row D	4	11	18	25	32		
Row E	5	12	19	26	33		
Row F	6	13	20	27	34		
Row G	7	14	21	28	35		

Key to your spiritual gift

Row A – Prophecy; **Row B** – Serving; **Row C** – Teaching; **Row D** – Stimulating the faith of others; **Row E** – Giving; **Row F** – Ruling or coordinating; **Row G** – Sympathy.

Once you have discovered your basic gifts – what next? Ask God to flood your life with His Holy Spirit so that you will become inwardly sensitive to the best gifts to expand and amplify your ministry. These gifts of the Spirit are described and defined in 1 Corinthians 12. If God, in His sovereignty, has ordained you to function in the role of an apostle, prophet, pastor, teacher or evangelist then this will become apparent to you through the recognition of those of your own local body, and by a spiritual witness to your own heart. Don't be over-concerned with aiming at being an apostle, prophet, pastor, teacher or evangelist. Concentrate on the depth of your ministry, and God will concentrate on the breadth.

Definition Gifts of God	Explanation	Dangers
1. Prophecy – or the God-given ability to present truth.	A persuasiveness and power in speech which brings to light things previously concealed.	**a.** Proud of rhetoric or persuasive speech. **b.** Dependent on ability to speak rather than on the Holy Spirit to convict. **c.** Seeing people as groups – not individuals. **d.** Judgmental and a sharp tongue without love.
2. Serving or demonstrating love by meeting practical needs so that others can be free for service.	An ability to detect personal needs; to overlook personal comfort so that the needs of others can be met. Romans 12:10	**a.** Proud of good deeds. **b.** Pushy or premature in attempting to meet the needs of others before they themselves realise what those needs are. **c.** Bitter when good deeds are not appreciated. **d.** Over-emphasis on practical – neglect of spiritual.
3. Teaching or clarifying truth by ensuring the accuracy of context etc.	An ability to research and unearth facts from Scripture, Romans 12:11. This involves diligence, fervency in study and careful research.	**a.** Boasting of knowledge one has accumulated. **b.** Concentration on details rather than principles. **c.** Captivated by research rather than responses. **d.** Believing truth is discerned through intellect.
4. Stimulating the faith of others in specific action towards definite goals.	An ability to counsel others and encourage them towards spiritual growth. Romans 12:12	**a.** Boasting about personal results. **b.** Discouraged when progress is slow. **c.** Indiscretion in sharing results. **d.** Giving too much time to the wrong people.
5. Giving or joyfully entrusting personal assets or possessions to others for the work of the ministry.	An ability to organise personal business; able to wisely invest and make quick and sound decisions about the right use of money.	**a.** Becoming proud of one's generosity. **b.** Measuring spiritual success by material gain. **c.** Attempting to buy influence with money. **d.** Overlooking long-range goals.
6. Ruling or co-ordinating the activities of others for the achievement of a common goal.	An ability to preside or lead; seeing future consequences of one's actions; able to distinguish major objectives and help others visualise them.	**a.** Proud of power over people. **b.** Using people to accomplish goals. **c.** Overlooking character faults in those who can be useful to reaching goals.
7. Empathising by an ability to identify with and comfort those in distress.	An ability to sympathise deeply with the misfortunes of others; mentally and emotionally relating and giving aid.	**a.** Proud of ability to sympathise. **b.** Resenting others who are not sympathetic to needs. **c.** Failing to be firm – guided by emotions, not logic.

Gifts of the Holy Spirit

1. *Tongues* – the ability to speak supernaturally in a language never learned.	Used in (a) congregational worship to bring a message from God or (b) privately as a devotional exercise.	**a.** Regarding 'tongues' as a mark of maturity. **b.** Proud of the prominence the gift inevitably brings.
2. *Interpretation of tongues* – the ability to supernaturally interpret a message given in tongues.	Used to interpret the mind of the Spirit as given through a message in other tongues.	**a.** Dependency on initiative. **b.** Over-zealousness in failing to develop sensitivity.
3. *Prophecy* – the ability to supernaturally convey God's message for the moment in the language of speaker and hearers.	Used to convey a message of edification, exhortation or comfort to God's people at specific times.	**a.** Interjecting personal feelings. **b.** Extending the ministry beyond limits. (Judgmental and harsh.)
4. *Word of knowledge* – a supernatural revelation to meet an emergency or crisis.	Used to supernaturally impart to a person or group a fact of knowledge which at that moment is otherwise unknown.	**a.** Hesitancy in communicating due to no logical explanation. **b.** Failure to exercise reason.
5. *Word of wisdom* – a supernatural revelation showing how to apply the right solution.	Used to supernaturally impart to someone the right procedure to take in a difficult situation.	**a.** Over-dependency on gifts. **b.** Lack of prayer and spiritual exercise.
6. *Faith* – the supernatural ability to visualise and witness spiritual achievement.	Used to supernaturally empower a person to 'believe' beyond their own natural faith.	**a.** Fear of being proved wrong. **b.** Ignoring others' feelings.
7. *Discerning of spirits* – the supernatural ability to discern the source of supernatural manifestations.	Used to detect the presence of evil spirits or to examine the source of manifestation which is dubious.	**a.** Seeing the problem not the person. **b.** Acting harshly – not firmly.
8. *Gift of healing* – the supernatural ability to bring God's healing power to the sick.	Used to bring deliverance to those bound in disease, infirmity, affliction etc.	**a.** Moving on one's initiative. **b.** Failure to develop sensitivity.
9. *Working of miracles* – the supernatural ability to suspend natural laws.	Used to bring God's power to bear upon a situation where natural means fail.	**a.** Pride in experience. **b.** Lack of prayer and devotion.

Gifts of Christ

1. *Apostle* – the gift of pioneering new territory for the gospel of Christ (example – a modern missionary).	This is a person in whom the gift of Christ dwells for the express purpose of making major in-roads with the gospel message.	**a.** Holding attention by virtue of one's position. **b.** Being proud because of personal selection.
2. *Prophet* – the gift of directing vision towards matters of vital concern in relation to immediate goals.	This is a person in whom the gift of Christ dwells for the purpose of elevating spiritual vision in the Body of Christ.	**a.** Attempting to move people by demand rather than love.
3. *Evangelist* – the gift of being able to point men and women to a saving knowledge of the Lord Jesus Christ.	This is a person in whom the gift of Christ dwells for the purpose of attracting large numbers of people to salvation in Christ.	**a.** Failure to recognise other related ministries. **b.** Relinquishing concern once converts have made a decision.
4. *Pastor* – the gift of being a shepherd to the flock of God.	This is a person in whom the gift of Christ dwells for the purpose of developing a group of believers into spiritual maturity.	**a.** Seeing only the needs of the local fellowship. **b.** Attempting to meet every need by personal effort.
5. *Teacher* – the gift of being able to expound the truths of God's Word in context and to make profound truths simple.	This is a person in whom the gift of Christ dwells for the purpose of edifying the Body of Christ in relation to the basic concepts of successful Christian living.	**a.** Expounding truth without applying principles. **b.** Becoming more interested in principles than people.

This appendix is also available in leaflet format, if you require further copies, and can be downloaded free from **www.cwr.org.uk/free-downloads**

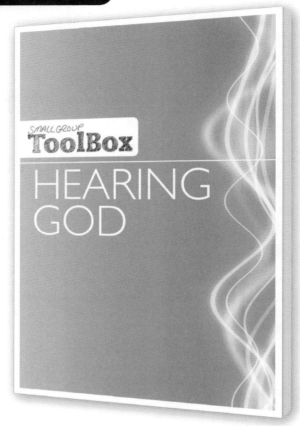

SMALLGROUP ToolBox

Hearing God is a subject that has long intrigued people – believers and non-believers alike. In this engaging new study guide, Ron Kallmier, addresses the issue squarely, asking: 'Does God speak to us today and if so, how?' Drawing on his own experiences in discerning the voice of God and his contagious passion for the Bible, this guide contains sections for personal reflection, group study, application and more.

- Ideal for use in small groups

48 pages, paperback, 148x210mm
ISBN: 978-1-85345-764-7

FAITH, HOPE, LOVE AND EVERYTHING IN BETWEEN

Life is a journey not a destination!

Although we don't all travel along the journey of discipleship at the same rate, there is a divine pattern at work which, whilst allowing the widest variety for each person and their own individuality, seeks to bring us closer to God through experiences which are common to us all.

This book will guide you into a deeper understanding of how the Lord will use every person, situation and circumstance in your life to make you more like Jesus.

156 pages, paperback, 153x230mm
ISBN: 978-1-85345-598-8

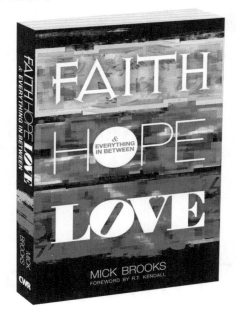

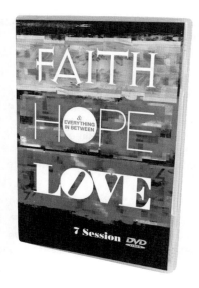

This seven-session DVD provides an honest explanation of the obstacles, opportunities and questions everyone encounters in their spiritual journey of discipleship. The sessions explore how we know God, what it means to be whole and holy and how to:

- Trust God amidst life's ambiguity and mystery
- Gain an eternal perspective
- Develop a closer relationship with God and others

and much more ...

Faith, Hope, Love and Everything in Between DVD
Presented by Mick Brooks
EAN: 5027957001329

For current prices visit www.cwr.org.uk/store
Available online or from Christian bookshops

Courses and seminars

Publishing and new media

Conference facilities

Transforming lives

CWR's vision is to enable people to experience personal transformation through applying God's Word to their lives and relationships.

Our Bible-based training and resources help people around the world to:
• Grow in their walk with God
• Understand and apply Scripture to their lives
• Resource themselves and their church
• Develop pastoral care and counselling skills
• Train for leadership
• Strengthen relationships, marriage and family life and much more.

Our insightful writers provide daily Bible-reading notes and other resources for all ages, and our experienced course designers and presenters have gained an international reputation for excellence and effectiveness.

CWR's Training and Conference Centre in Surrey, England, provides excellent facilities in an idyllic setting – ideal for both learning and spiritual refreshment.

CWR Applying God's Word
to everyday life and relationships

CWR, Waverley Abbey House,
Waverley Lane, Farnham,
Surrey GU9 8EP, UK

Telephone: **+44 (0)1252 784700**
Email: **info@cwr.org.uk**
Website: **www.cwr.org.uk**

Registered Charity No 294387
Company Registration No 1990308